REMARKABLE PEOPLE

Lady Gaga

by Anita Yasuda

MEDIA ENHANCED BOOKS AV² BY WEIGL ADDED VALUE • AUDIO VISUAL

www.av2books.com

Published by AV^2 by Weigl
350 5th Avenue, 59th Floor
New York, NY 10118

www.av2books.com www.weigl.com

Library of Congress Cataloging-in-Publication Data

Yasuda, Anita.
Lady Gaga / Anita Yasuda.
p. cm. -- (Remarkable people)
Includes index.
ISBN 978-1-61913-753-0 (hardcover : alk. paper) -- ISBN 978-1-61913-754-7 (softcover : alk. paper)
1. Lady Gaga--Juvenile literature. 2. Singers--United States--Biography--Juvenile literature. I. Title.
ML3930.L13Y37 2013
782.42164092--dc23
[B]

2012001328

Printed in the United States of America in North Mankato, Minnesota
1 2 3 4 5 6 7 8 9 0 16 15 14 13 12

062012
WEP170512

Editor: Heather Kissock
Design: Terry Paulhus

Photograph Credits
Weigl acknowledges Getty Images as the primary image supplier for this title.

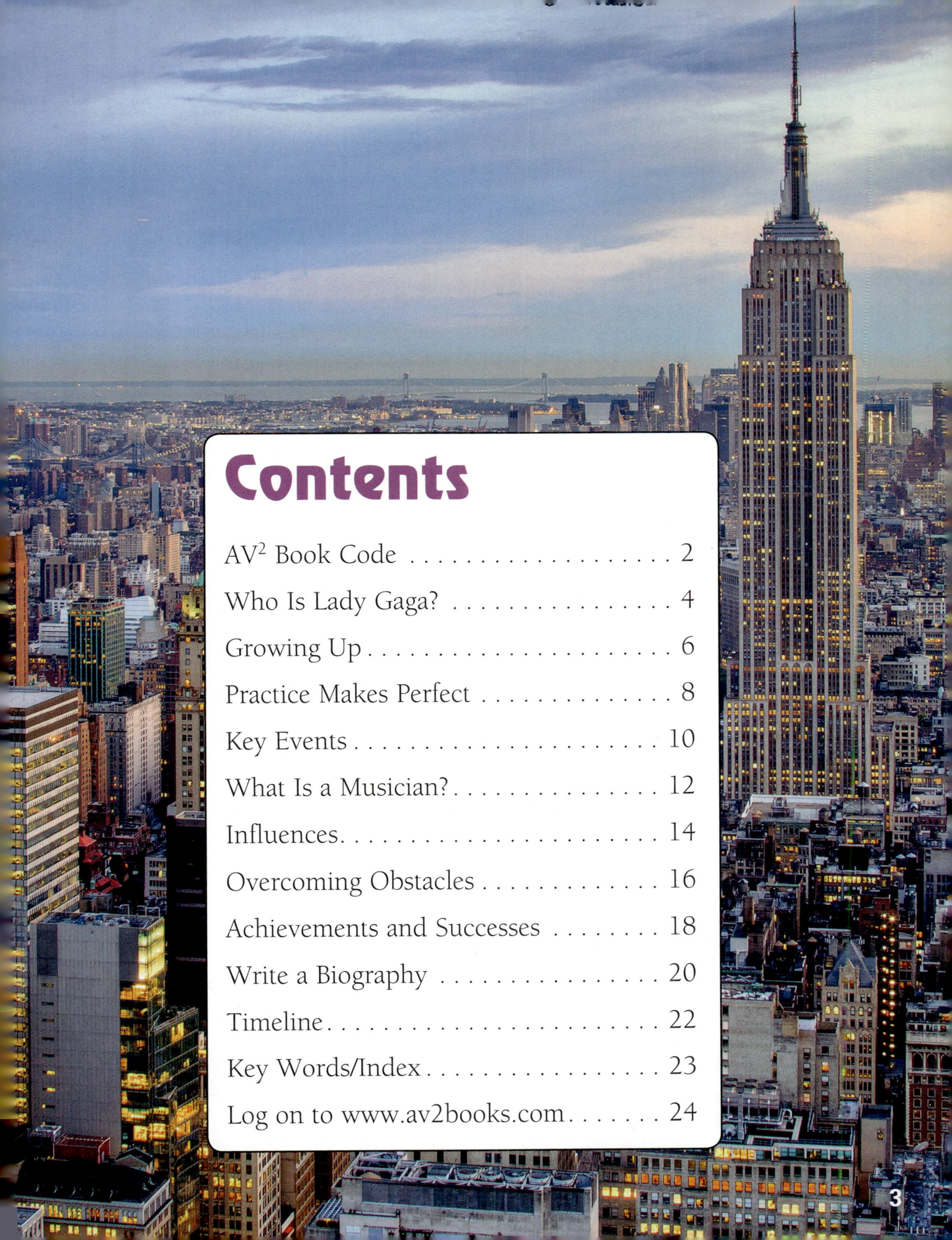

Contents

Who Is Lady Gaga?

Lady Gaga is one of the music industry's hardest-working entertainers. She is known for creating one-of-a-kind, live shows that combine music, dance, and fashion. When people go to a Lady Gaga concert, they see an artist who puts on a great show.

A talented performer, Lady Gaga released her first **studio album** in 2008. The Fame was a major success that included hit songs such as "Just Dance," "Poker Face," and "LoveGame." The album reached number two on the **Billboard 200**. Lady Gaga soon went on her first **headlining** tour. The tour lasted for six months, with Lady Gaga performing a total of 69 shows.

"You have to be unique, and different, and shine in your own way."

With more than 23 million albums and 64 million **singles** sold worldwide, Lady Gaga has become one of the best-selling artists of all time. This is an amazing accomplishment for such a young artist. Lady Gaga has used her success to bring attention to many causes, such as bullying and **self-acceptance**.

Growing Up

Lady Gaga was born on March 28, 1986, in New York City. Her parents, Joseph and Cynthia Germanotta, named her Stefani Joanne Angelina. Gaga has one younger sister, Natali. The family lived in Manhattan, one of New York's five **boroughs**.

Growing up, Lady Gaga loved music. Even as a baby, she liked to hear the sound of the family's piano being played. By age four, she had taught herself to play the piano. She wrote her first song, "Dollar Bills," at the same age.

Over the years, Gaga worked to develop her musical skills. To her family, friends, and teachers, Gaga was a determined artist who knew she wanted to perform. By age 11, she was taking full-day acting classes on weekends. At age 14, Gaga was performing in clubs around New York.

After teaching herself the basics of playing piano, Lady Gaga took lessons with a piano teacher to hone her skills.

Get to Know New York

FLOWER
Rose

TREE
Sugar Maple

BIRD
Bluebird

New York State is known as the Empire State. This nickname is thought to have come from President George Washington, who called New York the "seat of the empire."

Albany is New York State's capital city.

Every year, the Tony Awards are given out in New York City. The awards recognize excellence in **Broadway** theater.

Times Square is the heart of New York City. Found in central Manhattan, dozens of theaters, restaurants, and attractions are located here.

New York City is often referred to as the "entertainment capital of the world." How do you think growing up in a place known for its theaters, art galleries, and museums affected Lady Gaga? How did living in the city influence her music, clothing, and **ideals**?

Practice Makes Perfect

By the time she reached high school, music teachers were calling Gaga's voice "phenomenal." She often won leading roles in school musicals and could be seen playing Philia in *A Funny Thing Happened on the Way to the Forum* or Adelaide in *Guys and Dolls*. Gaga also joined a band that performed **covers** of classic rock songs.

At the age of 17, Gaga was selected for early admission into New York University's Tisch School of the Arts. Tisch is thought to be one of the United States' best **performing arts** schools. While at university, Gaga stood out with her bright, unusual clothing and strong vocals.

The Tisch School of the Arts was founded in 1965 to provide students with training in theater and film. Since then, the school has expanded its training programs to include dance, photography, and other artistic fields.

After a year at university, Gaga left to start her own band. She worked extremely hard at her music. Her efforts were rewarded when she was **signed** to Def Jam Recordings. This promising start ended when she was dropped from the label a short time later.

QUICK FACTS

- Gaga's stage name was inspired by a song called "Radio Ga Ga." The song was written and recorded by the rock group Queen.
- Gaga's sister, Natali, had a small part in her big sister's video for the song, "Telephone."
- Lady Gaga calls her fans "little monsters."

When Gaga was 20, she became a singer-pianist at **cabaret** clubs. Here, she impressed audiences with her stage presence and her amazing songwriting ability. Gaga also became known for her wild stage **antics**.

L.A. Reid was head of Def Jam Recordings when Lady Gaga was signed to the label. He has become well-known as a judge on *The X Factor*, a talent show for singers.

Key Events

Being dropped from Def Jam Recordings was a setback in Lady Gaga's career. She did not give up her dream, however. She worked even harder to establish herself as a serious artist. Gaga soon found another recording company that was interested in her music. In 2007, she signed with Interscope Records. There, Gaga worked as a songwriter, writing songs for Britney Spears, Fergie, and New Kids on the Block.

While working at Interscope, she attracted the attention of well-known singing star Akon. After hearing Gaga sing, Akon agreed to produce her debut album, The Fame. This was Lady Gaga's big break. The Fame went on to sell more than four million copies in the United States alone.

Akon is a successful recording artist in his own right. In 2010, *Forbes* Magazine ranked him as the third highest-paid rap artist in the world.

Thoughts from Lady Gaga

Lady Gaga loves being an artist and is very thankful for the opportunities she has had. Here are some comments Gaga has made about her fans, her success, and making music.

Gaga talks about how she relates to her fans.

"I love my little monsters. Now I live and create only for them."

Lady Gaga talks about life after her 2009 album The Fame was released.

"It's been a life-changing year for me creatively as a musician and a performance artist."

Gaga talks about the pressure she feels to create quality music.

"... I want to give my fans nothing less than the greatest album of the decade. I don't want to give them something trendy. I want to give them the future."

Gaga talks about being a celebrity.

"What I've learned is that you really don't need to be a celebrity or have money or have the **paparazzi** following you around to be famous."

Gaga discusses her work ethic.

"I am focused on the work. I am constantly creating. I am a busy girl. I live and breathe my work. I love what I do."

Gaga talks about working with Akon.

"He keeps me on my feet, very grounded, but he also puts me on a silver platter, which is always very nice."

What Is a Musician?

A musician is a person who can play an instrument, sing, or write music. Some musicians, such as Lady Gaga, can do all three. She showed she had a talent for music at a young age. It takes more than talent, however, to work in the music industry. A musician must **dedicate** hours to improving his or her skills.

Professional musicians spend hours practicing and rehearsing. Musicians work hard to write songs that express their feelings and entertain their fans. They work odd hours. Performances often take place at night and on weekends. Lady Gaga and many other musicians may only have one day off in a week. Some musicians tour nonstop. Tours can last a year or longer.

As well as touring, Lady Gaga often travels to foreign countries for special performances. In 2011, she sang at the MTV Europe Music Awards in Belfast, Northern Ireland.

Musicians 101

Justin Bieber (1994–)

Justin is a singer and musician. His mother posted videos of him performing on YouTube. Millions of people saw those videos, and Justin soon had a recording contract. In the spring of 2009, his first single, "One Time," came out. The album My World was released in November 2009 and went **platinum**. Justin followed the release of My World with My World 2.0. With this album, Justin became the youngest solo male performer since Stevie Wonder in 1963 to top the Billboard 200. In 2011, Justin was featured in the movie *Never Say Never*. It told the story of his rise to success.

Katy Perry (1984–)

Katy Perry is a songwriter and singer who was born in Santa Barbara, California. Growing up, Katy sang at her local church. After signing with Capitol Music Group in 2007, Katy began singing pop music. In 2008, Katy rose to fame with her single "I Kissed a Girl." The song went to the top of many music charts around the world. Her album, One of the Boys, featured several hits including "Hot N Cold." Katy became the first female artist to have five hits on the Billboard Hot 100 at the same time. Her next album, Teenage Dream, earned her six Grammy nominations and won her the MTV Music Awards for Video of the Year.

Taylor Swift (1989–)

Taylor is a singer and songwriter. She began her career when she was 11 years old, appearing at music clubs in Nashville before catching the attention of record companies. In 2006, her self-titled album went multi-platinum. She had three hit singles from this album, "Tim McGraw," "Teardrops on My Guitar," and "Our Song." In 2009, she won the Country Music Association's Entertainer of the Year Award. At the 2012 Grammy Awards, her song "Mean" won the award for Best Country Song.

Selena Gomez (1992–)

Selena is a musician and actor. She is best known for her role as Alex Russo on the Disney Channel Original Series, *Wizards of Waverly Place*. In 2008, Selena signed with Hollywood Records. The following year, she released her debut album Kiss & Tell. In 2010, Selena released her second album A Year Without Rain. It debuted in the fourth spot on the Billboard 200. Only one year later, Selena released her third album, When the Sun Goes Down. Selena won the Teen Choice Award for Best Love Song for "Love You Like a Long Song," one of the singles on the album.

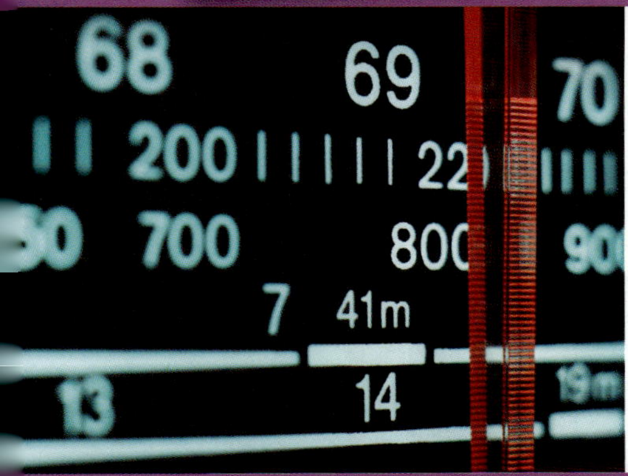

Billboard Charts

The Billboard charts are found in *Billboard* magazine. The charts rank a song's popularity. The more popular the song is, the lower the Billboard number. Every musician hopes to have a number one song on the Billboard charts. A song's popularity is judged by the number of times it is played on the radio, as well as the number of copies it sells.

Influences

Lady Gaga is known for creating spectacles. She does this by wearing outrageous clothing and staging dramatic concerts. Her musical idols are artists who are also known for bringing a high level of performance to their art.

One of Gaga's main influences is David Bowie. Bowie was part of the **glam rock** movement of the 1970s. Glam rock performers were known for their fashion just as much as their music. They wore loud clothing, makeup, and hairstyles. Their concerts often featured over-the-top performances. Bowie was one of the leading glam rockers of the time. He combined **image** and music to create amazing live shows.

During the glam rock era, David Bowie often appeared onstage as a character called Ziggy Stardust.

Like David Bowie, Gaga has combined fashion with music. She has been deeply influenced by designers, such as Alexander McQueen and Daphne Guinness, who are known for their dramatic clothing. By wearing clothes that are daring and original, Gaga has become a fashion **icon**. Fans and media alike look forward to seeing what Gaga is wearing.

THE GERMANOTTA FAMILY

Gaga's parents, Joseph and Cynthia, are very supportive of Gaga and her career. Though Gaga is constantly touring, she keeps in close contact with her family. Gaga stays at her family's Manhattan apartment when she is in New York City.

Cynthia and Joseph Germanotta often appear at events that are important to their daughter. In 2011, they attended the opening of a Christmas boutique that Lady Gaga developed in a New York department store.

Overcoming Obstacles

Gaga was not always popular. In school, other students often bullied her. They did not like the way she looked or dressed. Students often made fun of her for this reason.

The bullying upset Gaga, but she did not change the way she looked. Instead, she embraced her unique look and clothes. She used them to set herself apart from other performers. She now encourages others to celebrate their **individuality**.

Lady Gaga has become well-known for her willingness to take risks, in both her music and her fashion sense.

Today, Gaga supports anti-bullying programs. In 2011, she visited the White House to discuss bullying and how to stop it. She has sent messages of support to people who have been bullied, as well as those who speak against bullying in schools.

Gaga created the Born this Way Foundation to help young people gain confidence. The foundation shares its name with a Lady Gaga song. The song is about being happy with oneself. The goal of the foundation is to promote self-acceptance and respect. The foundation works to promote kindness and cooperation among people from all backgrounds.

Lady Gaga launched her Born This Way Foundation at Harvard University on February 29, 2012. Journalists and fans flocked to the university to hear her speak about the foundation's goals.

Achievements and Successes

Lady Gaga's music has brought her much success. This attention began as soon as her first album, The Fame, was released in October 2008. The album debuted in the Top 20, and two of the album's singles, "Just Dance" and "Poker Face," became number one hits. The Fame was nominated for five Grammy Awards and won the award for Best Electronic/Dance Album. "Poker Face" won the Grammy for Best Dance Recording. Another song on the album, "Paparazzi," won two MTV Video Music Awards.

In 2009, Gaga released her second album, The Fame Monster. She won the Grammy Award for Best Pop Vocal Album. At the MTV Music Awards, Gaga took home eight trophies. The video for the song "Bad Romance" earned Gaga the top prize of the night, Video of the Year.

Lady Gaga was named Best New Artist at the 2009 MTV Video Music Awards. She accepted the award from rapper Eminem and comedian Tracy Morgan.

In May 2011, Gaga released the song "Born this Way." It sold 1,108,000 copies in its first week. The single set a new iTunes record when it reached number one on the iTunes chart in less than three hours. Gaga ended 2011 by being voted Entertainer of the Year by the Associated Press. This award is given to the most influential person in entertainment and culture.

HELPING OTHERS

Often, musicians use their popularity to bring attention to a cause. They may bring attention to nonprofit organizations, environmental issues, or help fund special programs. Gaga has been involved with many charities and causes. Besides creating the Born This Way Foundation, Gaga is involved with Little Kids Rock. This national non-profit organization is dedicated to providing music education and musical instruments to public schools. Since 2002, Little Kids Rock has donated more than 30,000 instruments to schools across the United States. To learn more about this charity, visit littlekidsrock.org

Write a Biography

A person's life story can be the subject of a book. This kind of book is called a biography. Biographies describe the lives of remarkable people, such as those who have achieved great success or have done important things to help others. These people may be alive today, or they may have lived many years ago. Reading a biography can help you learn more about a remarkable person.

At school, you might be asked to write a biography. First, decide who you want to write about. You can choose a musician, such as Lady Gaga, or any other person. Then, find out if your library has any books about this person. Learn as much as you can about him or her. Write down the key events in this person's life. What was this person's childhood like? What has he or she accomplished? What are his or her goals? What makes this person special or unusual?

A concept web is a useful research tool. Read the questions in the following concept web. Answer the questions in your notebook. Your answers will help you write a biography.

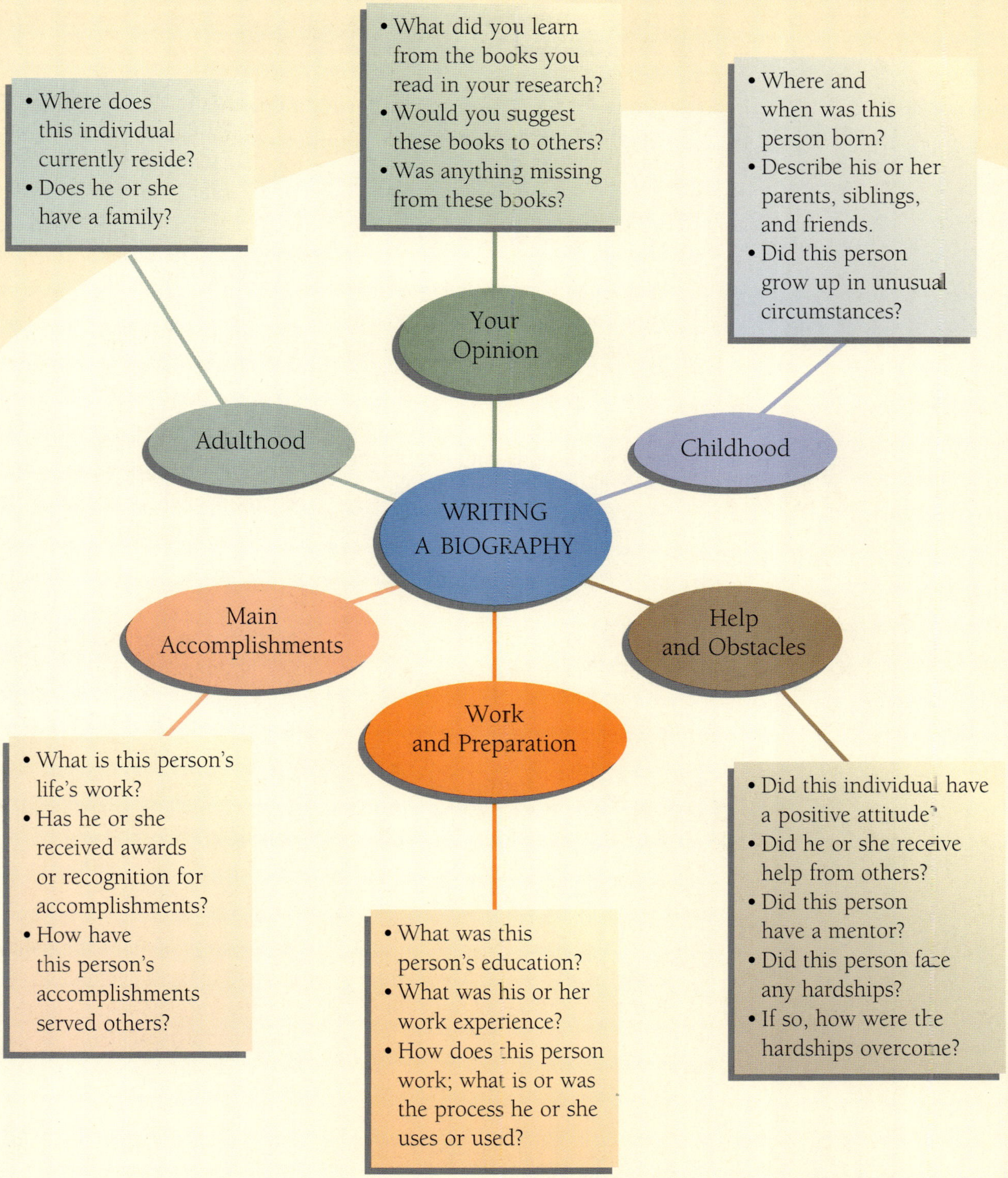
WRITING A BIOGRAPHY
Your Opinion
• What did you learn from the books you read in your research?
• Would you suggest these books to others?
• Was anything missing from these books?
Adulthood
• Where does this individual currently reside?
• Does he or she have a family?
Childhood
• Where and when was this person born?
• Describe his or her parents, siblings, and friends.
• Did this person grow up in unusual circumstances?
Main Accomplishments
• What is this person's life's work?
• Has he or she received awards or recognition for accomplishments?
• How have this person's accomplishments served others?
Work and Preparation
• What was this person's education?
• What was his or her work experience?
• How does this person work; what is or was the process he or she uses or used?
Help and Obstacles
• Did this individual have a positive attitude?
• Did he or she receive help from others?
• Did this person have a mentor?
• Did this person face any hardships?
• If so, how were the hardships overcome?

Timeline

YEAR	LADY GAGA	WORLD EVENTS
1986	Stefani Joanne Angelina Germanotta is born.	"We are the World," written by Michael Jackson and Lionel Ritchie, wins the Grammy for Song of the Year.
2003	Lady Gaga is accepted into New York University's Tisch School of the Arts.	Beyoncé's first solo album, *Dangerously in Love*, debuts at number one on the Billboard 200 chart.
2007	Lady Gaga signs with Interscope Records and begins working with Akon.	Live Earth, a worldwide series of concerts to raise awareness about climate change, takes place.
2008	Lady Gaga's first single, "Just Dance," is released.	Madonna celebrates her 50th birthday.
2009	Lady Gaga wins Best New Artist at the MTV Video Music Awards.	Taylor Swift's Fearless is the top-selling album of the year.
2011	Lady Gaga is voted Associated Press Entertainer of the Year.	Katy Perry becomes the only woman to have five number one singles from the same album on the Billboard Hot 100.
2012	Lady Gaga launches the Born This Way Foundation.	Justin Bieber releases his third studio album, Believe.

Key Words

antics: odd or amusing behavior

Billboard 200: a ranking of the 200 highest-selling music albums and songs in the United States

boroughs: small cities within larger cities

Broadway: the theater district in New York City

cabaret: a club or restaurant with entertainment

covers: performances of songs that were originally recorded by another artist

dedicate: to devote oneself wholly to a special purpose or cause

glam rock: a style of rock music made popular in the early 1970s that featured performers wearing dramatic clothes and makeup

headlining: performing as the star of the show

icon: the object of great attention and devotion

ideals: honorable principles or goals

image: how a person presents himself or herself

individuality: the qualities that make one person distinct from another

paparazzi: photographers who follow celebrities to take pictures for sale to magazines and newspapers

performing arts: the arts that are primarily performed before an audience, such as dance and drama

platinum: an award given to a musical artist who sells a million copies of a CD

self-acceptance: being happy with oneself despite flaws and weaknesses

signed: agreed to work with a music company for a set period of time or number of albums

singles: songs released to radio stations to play

studio album: a collection of songs recorded in a recording studio that are released in one package

Index

Log on to www.av2books.com

AV² by Weigl brings you media enhanced books that support active learning. Go to www.av2books.com, and enter the special code found on page 2 of this book. You will gain access to enriched and enhanced content that supplements and complements this book. Content includes video, audio, web links, quizzes, a slide show, and activities.

Audio
Listen to sections of the book read aloud.

Video
Watch informative video clips.

Embedded Weblinks
Gain additional information for research.

Try This!
Complete activities and hands-on experiments.

WHAT'S ONLINE?

Try This!

Complete an activity about your childhood.

Try this activity about key events.

Complete an activity about overcoming obstacles.

Write a biography.

Try this timeline activity.

Embedded Weblinks

Learn more about Lady Gaga's life.

Learn more about Lady Gaga's achievements.

Check out this site about Lady Gaga.

Video

Watch a video about Lady Gaga.

Check out another video about Lady Gaga.

EXTRA FEATURES

Audio
Listen to sections of the book read aloud.

Key Words
Study vocabulary, and complete a matching word activity.

Slide Show
View images and captions, and prepare a presentation.

Quizzes
Test your knowledge.

AV² was built to bridge the gap between print and digital. We encourage you to tell us what you like and what you want to see in the future.

Sign up to be an AV² Ambassador at www.av2books.com/ambassador.

Due to the dynamic nature of the Internet, some of the URLs and activities provided as part of AV² by Weigl may have changed or ceased to exist. AV² by Weigl accepts no responsibility for any such changes. All media enhanced books are regularly monitored to update addresses and sites in a timely manner. Contact AV² by Weigl at 1-866-649-3445 or av2books@weigl.com with any questions, comments, or feedback.

Cabriole

Pépite

Crapoto

Pullovère

Bermuda et Dandy

Luc Turlan

les amis de la FERME

CRAPOTO
ET LE BROYÉ DU POITOU

Geste éditions

Achevé d'imprimer à Barcelone en Espagne
sur les presses de Novoprint
en septembre 2008

ISBN : 978-2-84561-461-1 – LUP 633

Centre Routier
11, rue Norman-Borlaug
79260 La Crèche

www.gesteditions.com

L'hiver est arrivé et une neige immaculée recouvre la ferme.
Tout semble gelé, même la fumée qui sort lentement de la cheminée.
Crapoto ose quelques pas prudents dans ce paysage figé.

Cabriole et Peluchon sont déjà dehors.

– Viens nous aider, Crapoto ! On fait un bonhomme de neige !

Le cochon approche en grelottant.

– Facile à dire pour vous avec vos fourrures. Je n'ai pas un poil sur le dos, moi, je suis frigorifié ! Vraiment, je n'aime pas l'hiver !

– C'est vrai, approuve Peluchon, il fait un peu frais mais n'oublie pas que Noël approche.
– Oui, reprend Cabriole, pense au réveillon de ce soir !
Le visage de Crapoto s'illumine.
– Le réveillon ! Tu as raison ! Sapristi, vite, il faut faire une bûche de Noël !

Suivi de ses amis, Crapoto se précipite dans la cuisine.
– Le plus important, c'est le costume, explique-il en se coiffant d'une toque.
– J'ai un livre de cuisine, dit Cabriole.
Le cochon tourne les pages de la rubrique « desserts ».
– Voyons, Bananes flambées... Baba au rhum... Ah ! Bûche de Noël... Voilà la liste des ingrédients : farine, œufs, beurre, chocolat, levure, vanille, crème fraîche, fruits confits, sucre, sel.
– Allez, au travail !

Une rapide inspection dans les placards donne de bien maigres résultats. Il n'y a qu'un paquet de farine et un peu de sucre.

– Misère, ça ne suffira jamais pour faire notre bûche ! se lamente Cabriole.

– Je vais essayer de trouver ce qui manque, déclare Peluchon en sortant.

– On aura tout de même de quoi faire la décoration, remarque Crapoto. Je crois que j'ai trouvé des pépites de chocolat. Il faut les goûter pour voir.

Joignant le geste à la parole le goret en avale quelques-unes mais, aussitôt, il recrache en toussant.

– Beuârk ! Au secours, ça pique !

– Gros gourmand, s'amuse Cabriole, c'est du poivre en grains !

RINE
Sel

Peluchon est de retour.
– J'ai trouvé un peu de sel, un cadeau de mes cousins de l'île de Ré, et Pâquerette la vache a pu fournir le beurre. Sambon offre une tablette de chocolat puisque son régime le lui interdit.
– Je n'ai qu'un seul œuf à donner, déplore Plumette, mais je vais essayer d'en faire un autre avant ce soir !
– Beurre, sucre, farine, œuf, sel, chocolat... Il manque pas mal d'ingrédients, souligne la chèvre.
– On improvisera avec ce qu'on a, annonce Crapoto avec confiance. Commençons par faire chauffer le four et sortons les ustensiles !

La cuisine se transforme rapidement en un vaste chantier où Crapoto s'affaire dans tous les sens.

– Tu n'as pas besoin d'une balance ou d'un verre doseur ?

– Inutile ! Un vrai chef cuisine d'instinct ! dit-il en mélangeant les ingrédients énergiquement.

Soudain, Cabriole s'inquiète.
– Où est passé le chocolat ?
– Euh... Je l'ai beaucoup goûté, avoue le cochon, il n'y en a plus... Mais qu'importe, pas besoin de chocolat !

Bientôt le gâteau paraît prêt. Peluchon ouvre le four en faisant attention à la chaleur.

– Zut, la bûche est trop haute. Elle n'entrera pas dans le four !

– Bah... je vais l'aplatir un peu et ça ira, dit Crapoto en écrasant la préparation.

– Attendez ! s'écrie tout à coup Plumette, voilà un autre œuf tout frais. Je viens de le pondre.

– Trop tard, on a fini.

– Tant pis, je vais l'étaler dessus, ça donnera du goût ! décrète le chef débutant.

Pendant la cuisson du gâteau, on ne reste pas inoccupé car c'est le moment d'agrémenter la salle à manger. Chacun apporte sa touche de fantaisie personnelle au décor.
Quelques guirlandes, du houx bien disposé et la maison prend tout de suite un air de fête.
Ensuite, il faut dresser la table.
– Attention, précise Cabriole, le couteau à droite et la fourchette à gauche de l'assiette.
Pendant ce temps, une bonne odeur a doucement envahi la cuisine.
Il va être l'heure de sortir la bûche du four.
– Préparez vos assiettes !

Mais... surprise ! La bûche n'a pas gonflé comme l'aurait voulu Crapoto. Au lieu d'un beau gâteau rebondi, Crapoto sort du four une galette toute plate ! Quelle déception !

– On pourrait recommencer, suggère Plumette.

– Impossible, il ne reste qu'un peu de sucre en poudre.
– Même pas, dit Crapoto, je l'ai mangé en rangeant la cuisine.
Le cochon a l'air si déçu que personne ne songe à le blâmer.

– Goûtons tout de même ce gâteau, propose Peluchon. Il sent bon et il a une belle couleur dorée !
Hélas, la galette est beaucoup trop dure. Cabriole essaie de la couper avec un couteau. Impossible !
– Pousse-toi, dit Crapoto en colère, je vais le partager, moi, ce fichu dessert !
Sous le regard médusé de ses amis, il donne alors un grand coup de poing au centre de la galette qui se brise en petits morceaux.
– Bravo ! applaudit le baudet. Il n'y a plus qu'à se régaler !
Mais personne n'ose prendre la première bouchée.

Peluchon finit par attraper un petit fragment
de gâteau et le croque du bout des dents.
Les autres le regardent avec appréhension...
Un goût suave lui emplit la bouche.
– Hmmm... c'est excellent ! dit-il.

Cabriole essaie aussi, puis Plumette et Pullovère goûtent à leur tour.

– C'est une vraie réussite, Crapoto !

– Il n'empêche que je suis déçu, je voulais faire une bûche.

– Ne te lamente pas, ce gâteau est vraiment très bon, la preuve, on a presque tout mangé !

La fête se poursuit très tard et le moment est venu de se coucher. Après cette soirée animée, le calme revient dans la petite ferme du Poitou et chacun s'endort paisiblement. Soudain, un murmure trouble le silence de la nuit...

– Peluchon ? Tu entends ? Il y a quelqu'un dans la cuisine, chuchote Crapoto effrayé.

Le baudet et le cochon s'approchent prudemment de la cuisine et écoutent à travers la porte. Manifestement, il y a un intrus dans la maison. Ils entrouvrent délicatement le battant. Près de la cheminée un homme leur tourne le dos. Habillé tout en rouge, il est aussitôt reconnu par les deux amis.

– Oh ! Le Père Noël ! s'exclame Crapoto.

– Bonsoir, répond le vieil homme d'une voix douce, je suis désolé de vous avoir réveillés. En voyant ce restant de galette je n'ai pas pu résister à l'envie d'en manger.

Crapoto reste bouche bée.

Le Père Noël poursuit :

– Pourriez-vous me donner la recette ? Je suis sûr que mes lutins se régaleront autant que moi. J'aimerais leur faire cette surprise.

THE

– Bien sûr, balbutie Crapoto en se redressant fièrement. Je vais vous expliquer. C'est très simple...
Il se lance alors dans un exposé détaillé de la recette qu'il a inventée grâce au hasard.

Le Père Noël note soigneusement les indications du petit cochon.
– Et comment pourrait-on appeler cette galette ? demande-t-il.
– Un BROYÉ ! propose Peluchon, puisque c'est le seul moyen de le partager.
– Je m'en souviendrai, dit en riant le Père Noël.

– Je dois partir maintenant, reprend le Père Noël. J'ai une longue tournée à finir, je penserai à vous chaque fois que je mangerai du broyé. Au revoir et merci !
En un instant, son traîneau s'élance avec légèreté vers le ciel étoilé.
Émerveillés, Peluchon et Crapoto restent un long moment devant ce spectacle magique. Un cri de Plumette les ramène à la réalité.
– Vite ! Venez tous ! Venez voir !

La poule tout excitée danse devant une montagne
de cadeaux multicolores.
Peluchon et Crapoto échangent un regard complice.
– Regardez ! clame
Plumette. Le Père Noël !
Le Père Noël est passé !

Le Broyé du Poitou

pour 6 personnes

Mélange dans une terrine 500g de farine, 250g de sucre, 250g de beurre mou, 1 oeuf, 1 pincée de gros sel.
Beurre un moule et étale la pâte à la main.
Utilise un pinceau pour dorer la galette avec un jaune d'oeuf.
Tu peux faire des dessins avec une fourchette.
Demande à un adulte de faire cuire ton broyé 25 minutes environ à 200°C.

Bon appétit

Trapoto

Plume
Sambon
Peluchon
Labour
Bourguig

1

Pour Stan
V. F.
Pour Amelia Edwards
avec toute mon affection
D. K.

Première édition française 2002 par Éditions Gründ

ISBN : 2-7000-4867-9
Dépôt légal : janvier 2002
Édition originale 2002 par Walker Books Ltd,
sous le titre *To mum with love*

Secrétariat d'édition et PAO : Jérémie Salinger
Texte composé en Minion Condensed, Kidprint MT et Maboul Divin,
titres en Garamome Divin
Imprimé à Hongkong
www.grund.fr

Loi n° 49-956 du 16 juillet 1949 sur les publications
destinées à la jeunesse.

Éditions Gründ – 60, rue Mazarine – 75006 Paris

Bon anniversaire Maman

Texte
Vivian French
Illustrations
Dana Kubick
Adaptation française
Emmanuel Pailler

Gründ

Demain c'est l'anniversaire de Maman. Théo va trouver son grand frère Max.

– Qu'est-ce que tu vas offrir à Maman pour son anniversaire ? lui demande-t-il.

– Des fleurs,
répond Max.
Maman aime
beaucoup les
fleurs.
– Bonne idée !
s’écrie Théo,
et il court dans
le jardin.

Théo cueille…

les cinq plus belles…

fleurs…

du jardin.

Mais sur le chemin du retour, les fleurs ont perdu leurs pétales !
– Dommage, dit Théo tout triste, avec les oreilles tombantes.

Alors Théo va trouver sa grande sœur Cannelle. Elle est occupée à compter les pièces de sa tirelire.

– C'est pour l'anniversaire de Maman ? demande-t-il.

– Oui, répond Cannelle. Je vais lui offrir une boîte de bonbons.

– Super ! s’écrie Théo, et il court chercher sa tirelire.

Théo grimpe sur
le fauteuil…

pour atteindre
sa tirelire…

et offrir lui aussi des
bonbons à sa maman.

Mais quand la
tirelire s'ouvre…

patatras !
Il n'y a qu'une seule
pièce de puzzle
à l'intérieur.
– Dommage, dit Théo
tout triste, avec les
moustaches tombantes.

Alors Théo va trouver sa grande sœur Cléo dans la cuisine.

– Et toi, qu'est-ce que tu fais pour l'anniversaire de Maman ? lui demande-t-il.

– Je prépare un gâteau d'anniversaire, répond Cléo.

– Youpi ! Quelle
bonne idée,
s'écrie Théo,
et il sort de
la cuisine en
faisant la roue.

Théo fait un beau …

gâteau…

en glaise !

Mais, splatch !
le gâteau tombe
par terre…
– Dommage, dit
Théo tout triste,
avec la queue
tombante.

Théo monte dans sa chambre chercher un autre cadeau pour sa maman. Il regarde dans son carton plein de voitures, mais elles sont toutes abîmées. Sa sœur Cléo ouvre alors la porte :

– C'est l'heure d'aller au lit, Maman l'a dit.

Cette nuit-là, Théo ne dort pas très bien.

Le lendemain matin, Cléo, Cannelle et Max viennent voir Théo dans sa chambre.

– Qu'est-ce qui ne va pas ? demande Max à Théo.

– Je n'ai pas trouvé de cadeau pour Maman, répond Théo.

– Tu n'as qu'à lui donner un baiser, dit Cléo. C'est ce que Maman préfère.

Théo bondit sur son lit.
– Ça y est ! J'ai trouvé ! s'écrie-t-il. Je sais ce que je vais lui offrir.
– Tu viens ? demande Cannelle.
– J'arrive tout de suite, répond Théo.

Cléo, Cannelle et Max
descendent donner leur
cadeau à Maman.

– Oh, des fleurs ! dit Maman. Comme elles sont belles ! Et mes bonbons préférés ! Et quel gâteau magnifique ! Mais… où est Théo ?

Tout à coup…

Théo apparaît, avec une grande boîte en carton dans les bras.

– BON ANNIVERSAIRE MAMAN ! dit-il.

– Oh, des fleurs ! dit Maman. Comme elles sont belles ! Et mes bonbons préférés ! Et quel gâteau magnifique ! Mais… où est Théo ?

Tout à coup…

Théo apparaît, avec une grande boîte en carton dans les bras.
– BON ANNIVERSAIRE MAMAN ! dit-il.

Maman commence
à ouvrir la boîte.
– Mais, Théo, disent
ensemble Max, Cléo et
Cannelle étonnés, il n’y a
rien à l’intérieur !

– Mais si ! répond Théo. C’est une boîte pleine de bisous.
– Oh, Théo, quel merveilleux cadeau ! dit Maman en l’embrassant sur le nez.
– Attention à ne pas la vider tout de suite, dit Max.
Maman sourit.
– Oh non ! Les boîtes à bisous ne se vident jamais.

– C'est vrai, dit Théo. Elles ne se vident jamais, jamais, JAMAIS ! Mais tout de même, il donne à sa maman un autre bisou – on ne sait jamais !